North-South Pendulum Golf Swing

By: Lee Adger

ROYSTON
Publishing

BK Royston Publishing
P. O. Box 4321
Jeffersonville, IN 47131
502-802-5385
http://www.bkroystonpublishing.com
bkroystonpublishing@gmail.com

© Copyright – 2019

All Rights Reserved. No part of this book may be reproduced, stored in a retrieval system, or transmitted by any means without the written permission of the author.

Cover Design: Gad Savage – Elite Covers
Cover Image © Lee Adger

ISBN: 978-1-946111-85-2

Printed in the United States of America

Prelude

The encouragement to write this book came from a good friend of mine, professional basketball player and Coach Johnny Davis.

The technique explained and steps illustrated in this book will improve the golfer's swing by 90%.

My students and golf partners have shown significant improvement each time out because this winning concept is designed to perfect your swing as well as your overall golf game.

The North – South Pendulum Swing can only be topped by the golf industry's Iron Byron and the mechanical ball hitting machine.

You will come away with a better knowledge of the golf swing.

Fore Thought

If you allow golf tradition to pollute the "pendulum truths" found throughout this book, then the truths could become ineffective in helping you to master this simple swing and not give you the opportunity to fully enjoy the game of golf.

Making the word of God of none effect through your tradition, which ye have delivered: and many such like things do ye.

Mark 7:13

Acknowledgements

My thanks to Coach Davis for continually reminding me to keep good notes because I needed to share my knowledge of the golf swing with the world.

Thanks to Marshall Higginbothum a young student in pursuit of his dream, whom I've known from age 8 and now in college.

After hundreds of text messages, emails and countless hours on the phone and Skype with Coach Davis and Marshall who have been relentless in seeking knowledge, I feel that it's time to put it in print.

My many thanks to another good friend, mentor and business partner, Champion Tour player Clyde Hughey who was the 2000 driving distance leader.

Since connecting with Clyde in 2010, he has openly shared all of the intricate details of his swing with me.

Clyde worked years with legendary teacher Joe Norwood and has mastered the ONLY TRUE PENDULUM SWING that I have ever seen and analyzed.

Thanks to Debbie Ray, Jacqueline Odom, Don McMillian, and my wife Dee for all of their input and assistance to help me complete this project.

Table of Contents

Prelude	iii
Fore Thought	iv
Acknowledgements	v

The North – South Difference — 1

Balance — 3

The Secret is 1+1+1=1 — 5

Overview — 7

Blueprint — 9

Putting
- Stance — 13
- Grip — 14
- Setup — 18
- Stroke & Focus Point — 22
- Chipping Setup & Swing — 23

Full Swing
- Feet position — 29
- Key to Stability — 30

Swing Grip
- Lead hand — 31
- Trail hand — 33

Swing Setup	**35**
Swing Positions / Check points	**41**
Clubhead Real vs. Feel	**45**
Pendulum Bunker	
Swing Axis & Low Point	**47**
Bunker Swing	**48**
Drills	
Trail Arm Range of Motion	**53**
Trail Arm Movement	**56**
Feet Square to the Toe Line	**60**
Trail Book Back to the Toe Line	**68**
Lead Arm Seated	**77**
Trail Arm Seated	**79**
Both Arms Seated	**81**
Both Arms Standing	**83**
Half Shaft	**85**
Putting Balance	**89**
Chipping Balance	**91**
Swing Path	**93**
Final Thought	**107**
Glossary	**109**

The North-South Difference

North – South Pendulum Swing is so named because the golf club is swung on a more vertical swing path.
North being up toward the sky and **south** being down toward the ground.

This swing differs from the traditional swing in that **all angles are pre-set at the address setup position**.

The pre-set angles eliminate excess movement, rotation during the swing and reduce stress in the lower lumbar area, allowing for **a repeatable swing on a pre-defined path** with effortless **power generated from three combined sources; centrifugal force, gravity and the booster muscle**. *(See Glossary)*

Balance

The KEY to consistency in golf is a simplistic understanding of how to keep your center of gravity as stable as possible from setup to the impact position.

By moving the center of gravity closer to the arch of the trail foot at the address setup position, at least 70% of the weight is on the trail side of the body for the full swing.
This provides perfect balance and stability upon the Base of Support and frees the mind to perform the single task of swinging with minimal thought or effort.

To pre-set the body in a position to remain quiet during the swing, move the trail foot back from the toe line and turn the chest just enough to align the shoulders toward the target.

The upper torso should be pre-rotated and balanced so **there is no need for rotation during the swing**.

A quieter body promotes a quieter mind.

The Secret is
1 + 1 + 1 = 1

The secret is comprised of three parts.
The secret is 1+1+1 = 1.

The first 1 is to achieve the one and only **feeling** that eliminate mechanical thinking on every swing.
The **feeling** begins with the lead hand grip (pg... 21) making the arm an extension of the club thereby establishing the pendulum rod.

The second 1 is to understand how to position the feet and body so that perfect balance and stability is maintained throughout the entire swing.

The third 1 is to understand the **pre-defined swing path** and how to swing without any manipulation.
Once the pendulum rod is established it moves on a defined path. (See Drill pg... 93)
Adding the trail hand and arm will enhance the pendulum movement and not alter it while providing **effortless power** by conserving not exerting and wasting energy. (See grip pg... 31-34)

Combine these three steps and the ultimate swing can be achieved.

OVERVIEW

The North – South pendulum golf swing is derived from the folding and unfolding of the trail elbow allowing the golf club to be swung on an up and down path and operates on the principle of a true pendulum moving on a fixed point.

(Fulcrum... see pictures)

The individual is able to maintain perfect Balance and Stability from address to impact by establishing a fixed Line of Gravity and a high lead side FIXED POINT for the golf swing. Doing this minimizes excess movement and reduces stress on the body.

Blueprint

The North – South Blueprint refers to the step by step process which is designed to build your swing from the ground up.

With one simple grip for every club from putter to driver and one full swing motion for every part of the game, including bunker play.

Foundation (Lower torso)

For a balanced and stable setup from putter to driver the key is to have the lead foot turned toward the target and the trail foot back from the toe line.

(The Feet are never square to the toe line.)

Sneak Peek into my putting stance

Sneak Peek into my full swing stance.

Blueprint

The solid Base of Support is positioned in such a way that stress on the body is minimized.

Turn the Lead foot 30-45 degrees toward the target.

Move the trail foot back from the toe line (3" minimum) and feel the weight shift.

Post
The trail leg supports and provides leverage for the swing. Sit down on the Trail leg to pre-load weight for the full swing.

Prop
The lead leg braces the Post for stability.
  (Lead knee/thigh inward toward the trail big toe)

Framework (Upper torso)

Pendulum
The lead arm and golf club form a fixed axis Pendulum unit that moves on a pre-defined swing path with a consistent low point.

Power
The trail arm supplies the movement and Power.
The pendulum rod is moved with a trail elbow fold / unfold and downswing power is from the booster muscle.

Blueprint

Posture

The upper torso is positioned in a way to achieve perfect balance so that **no head or body movement is felt from setup to the impact position**.

Finished Product Position 0 (Address)

(See picture pg 39)

Upper torso turned so that the LOG is close to the trail foot.
Bend forward at the hips with lead shoulder higher.

(Center of the chest turned 10 degrees / 6 inches to the rear from center)
      (Core is Pre-rotated & trail glute is Pre-loaded)

Putting Stance

Feet are angled toward the target and the width varies depending on individual comfort level.

The lead foot is 45 degrees & Trail foot 55 degrees.
(Photo below)

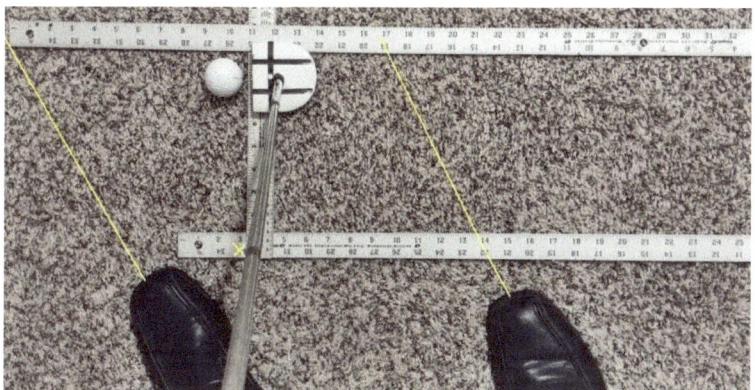

Sneak Peek into **MY** setup.
- **Lead foot turned at an angle about 9" in front of the ball.**
- **Trail foot back 1" from the toe line & turned at an angle about 6" behind the ball.**
- **Stance width minimum is 14 inches.**
- **Putter ½ inch behind the ball.**
- **From MY view point the shaft should be about 3" from the big toe.**

Establishing a precise setup routine will eliminate guess work and allow for a repeatable stroke.

Putting Grip

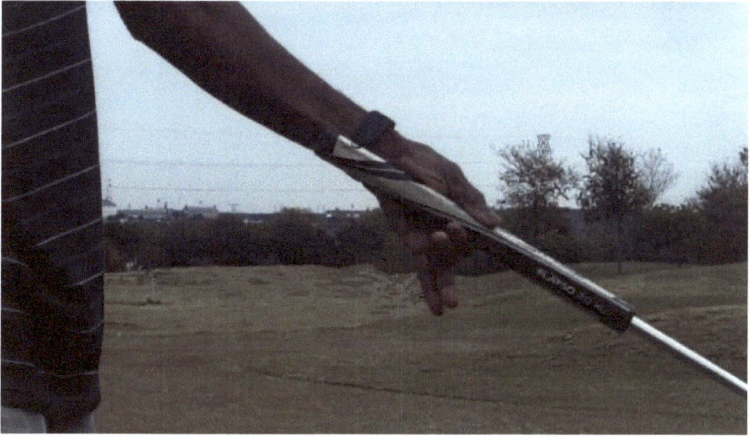

The grip rest on the palm joint / pad of the lead forefinger and under the thumb pad.
(Feel that lead Thumb Nail connects to the Sweet Spot of the putter.)

Putting Grip

A short thumb applies pressure at about a 7 to lock and Supinate the wrist to activate the forearm muscles, making the putter and arm a one piece pendulum rod.

With the lead elbow bent and upper arm to the side in the socket, the pendulum will freely swing at the shoulder socket like a door hinge.

The grip rest on the 1ˢᵗ joint / pad of the trail forefinger and the thumb pad sits perfectly down on the lead thumb. **Firming the pressure to 6 will set the trail wrist down / forward to seal the wrists.**

Putting Setup

The grip rest on the palm joint / pad of the lead forefinger and under the thumb pad. (For Leverage)

A short thumb applies pressure at 7 to lock, Supinate and set the wrist down to activate the forearm muscles, making the putter and arm a one piece pendulum rod.

Putting Setup

Bend the elbow to lift the putter and feel the leverage.

Turn the feet toward the target with weight 70% on the lead leg. **Moving the body weight forward will lean the shaft about 1.5 inches to deloft the putter and position the trail thumb at an angle to push away into the elbow so that there is a delay at the end of the back stroke.**

(See pg... 19)

Putting Setup

The grip rest on the 1st joint / pad of the trail forefinger and the thumb pad sits perfectly down on the lead thumb.

At the conclusion of the putting setup the Lead arm will naturally hang down with the hand in front of the thigh establishing a pendulum axis and the low point for a repeatable putting stroke.

Putting Stroke & Focus Point

Firm pressure with the lead thumb and forefinger will allow you to feel the club and a rigid arm as a one piece unit.

When the trail hand is added the putting stroke is made with **a piston action of the trail elbow** feeling slightly up going back and down through impact.

(Feel the delay)

The end of the back stroke is when a slight resistance is felt in the trail elbow & tricep.

The end of the through stroke is when the trail arm is completely straight.

Chipping Setup & Swing

Rest the grip on the forefinger palm joint.

Apply pressure at 8-9 with the tip of a short thumb to activate the forearm muscles.

Chipping Setup & Swing

Turn the lead foot out 45 degrees toward the target.

Move the trail foot back from the toe line a minimum of 3 inches and turned toward the target.

Chipping Setup & Swing

Apply pressure at 8 with the tip of the trail thumb on the target side of the grip.

Place 70% of your weight on the lead leg and extend down to the ball.

Chipping Setup & Swing

Swing back by folding the trail elbow with no wrist action.

Unfold the trail elbow allowing the club to go down through the impact zone and the low point.

Chipping Setup & Swing

Finish in the same balanced position that was established at setup.

Full Swing
Feet Position

Setting the trail foot a minimum of 3 inches back from the toe line will:
- Reduce stress in the lower lumbar area.
- Position the base of support for stability and balance.
- Allow for a natural inside to out swing path.
- Allow the trail leg to be used a post during the backswing.

Turning the Lead foot out 45 degrees toward the target will:
- Allow the **knee to be set as a brace** for the post.
- Allow the weight to move toward the toes of the lead foot on the downswing.

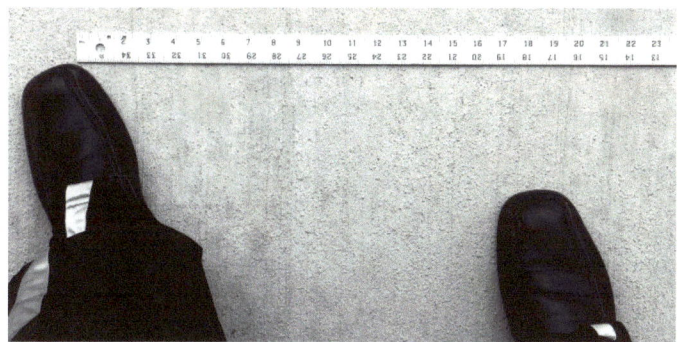

Sneak peek into **MY** stance width.

For me to stay in balance and allow my arms to swing under my chest, my stance width is:
Minimum width = 13" Maximum width = 17"

Full Swing
Key to Stability

The key to maintaining stability and balance during the full swing is to pre-load weight on the trail leg with the outside of the hip at the inside of the heel.

Swing Grip
Lead Hand

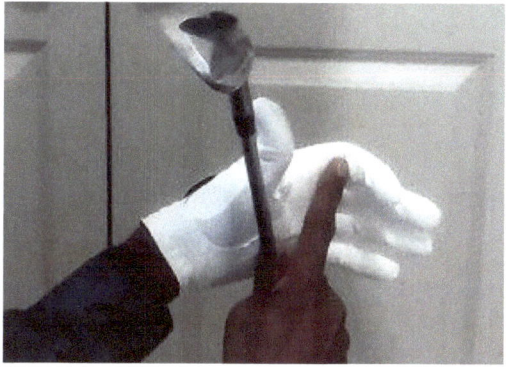

The grip rest on the palm joint / pad of the lead forefinger.

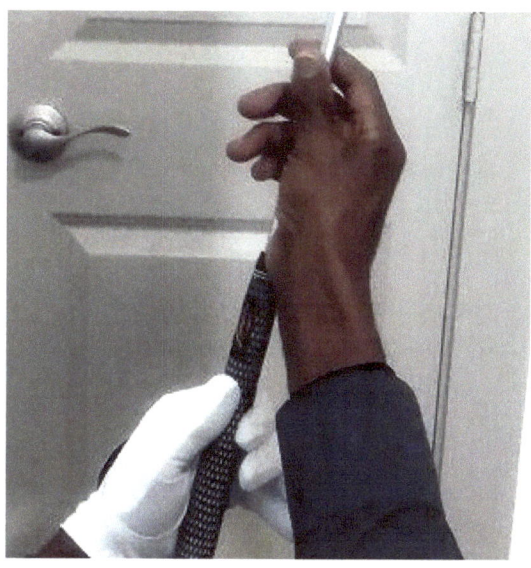

Apply pressure at 8-9 with a short thumb to activate the forearm muscles.

Swing Grip
Lead Hand

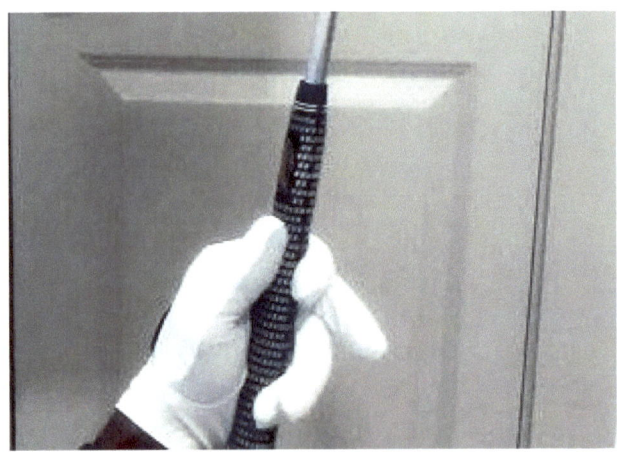

Lock the wrist with the pinky finger.

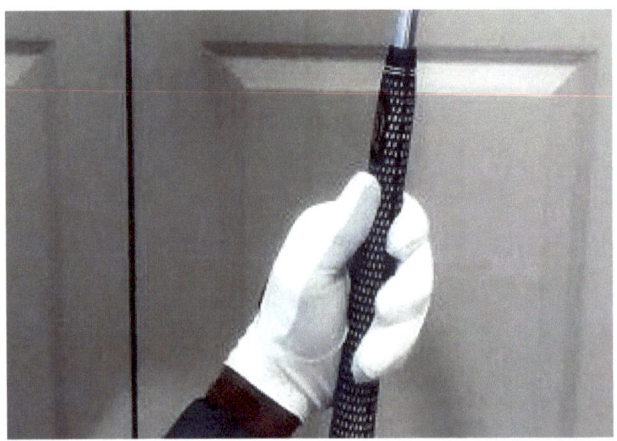

Lay the two middle fingers on the grip for support.

Swing Grip
Trail Hand

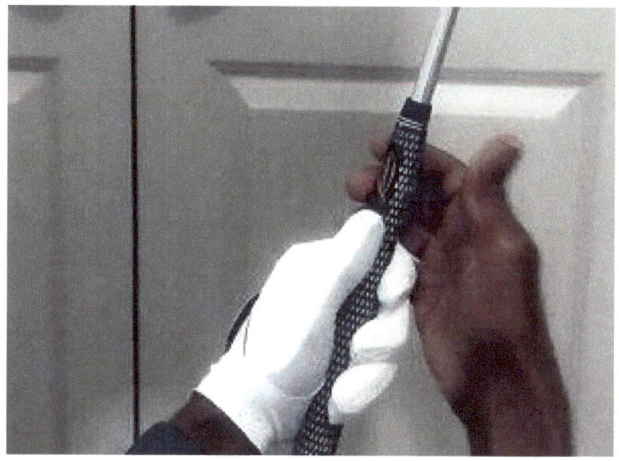

The grip rest on the 1st joint / pad of the trail forefinger.

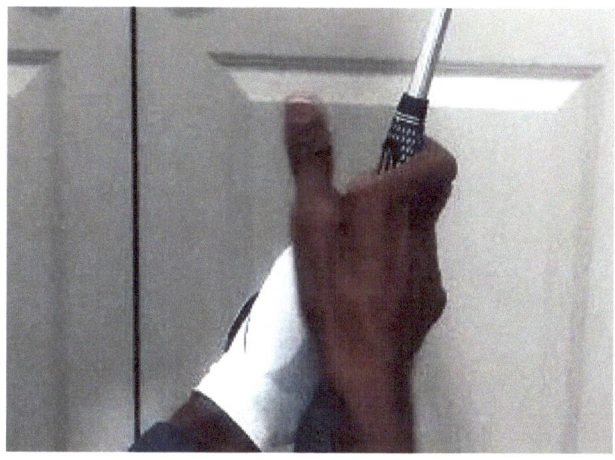

Allow the thumb pad to cover the lead thumb.

Swing Grip
Trail Hand

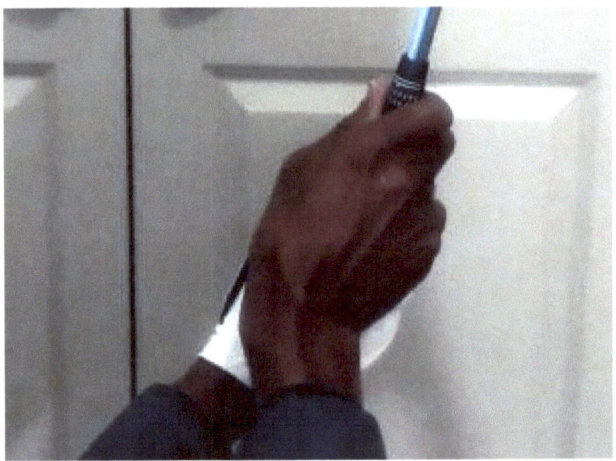

To maximum hood *(See Glossary)* the trail hand, apply pressure at 7-8 with tip of the thumb on the target side of the grip.

Swing Setup

Step 1

Rest the grip on the forefinger palm joint.

Step 2

Apply pressure at 8-9 with the tip of a short thumb to activate the forearm muscles.

Swing Setup

Step 3

Turn the lead foot out 45 degrees toward the target.

Step 4

Move the trail foot back from the toe line a minimum of 3 inches.

Swing Setup

Step 5

Apply pressure at 8 with the Tip of the Trail thumb on the target side of the grip.

Step 6

Turn the chest to align the shoulders toward the target.

Swing Setup

Step 7

Sit down on the Trail leg / hip for balance and stability. Extend down to the ball and **relax the trail elbow**.

Swing Setup

At the conclusion of the swing setup the Lead arm will naturally hang down with the hand in front of the thigh establishing a pendulum axis and the low point. By keeping the hands in front of the thigh at address *(never in the center of the body)*, the low point will be consistent. All clubs from wedge to driver will setup with the hands ahead of the clubface *(shaft lean)*, allowing for easy ball placement based on the low point.

Swing positions / check points

There are 6 positions / check points in the swing.
1. Shaft is parallel to the ground.
2. Trail forearm is parallel to the ground and shaft vertical.
3. Trail arm has folded to the max.
4. Shaft is parallel to the ground.
5. Post impact where the hand is just past the lead thigh.
6. Shaft is vertical with hand above the shoulder.

(Lead elbow starting to bend at position 5 will allow the shaft to go vertical)

Position 0 = Address setup position.

Swing Positions

Position 1 = Club shaft is parallel to the ground.
(Over the toe line)

Position 2 = Lead forearm is parallel to the ground.

Swing Positions

Position 3 = End of the backswing.

Position 4 = Club shaft is parallel to the ground.

Swing Positions

Position 5 = Post impact.
(Lead elbow starting to bend at position 5 will allow the shaft to go vertical) *** MAJOR KEY ****

Position 6 = Back of the lead hand faces the target.

Clubhead Real vs. Feel

A **Sneak Peak** into the real vs. feel of **MY** clubhead.

From my view point when my hands are about waist high in the backswing the toe of the club feels down to the ground. *(See picture 2)*

1

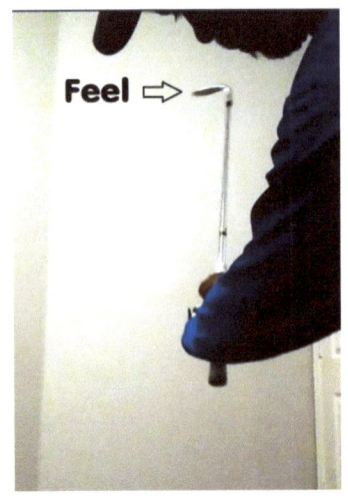 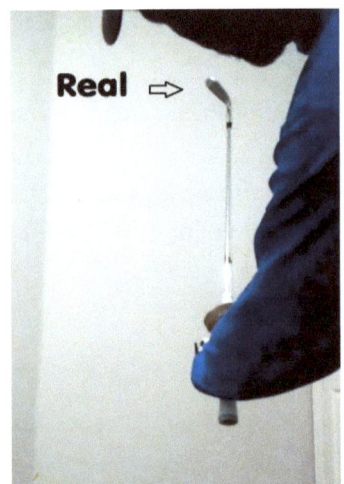

2   3

Pendulum Bunker Swing
Axis & Low Point

Bunker Swing

Swing Position 0

Set the pendulum low point behind the ball.

Swing Position 1

Bunker Swing

Swing Position 3

Swing Position 4

Bunker Swing

Swing Position 5

Swing through the low point.

Bunker Swing

Swing Position 6

Back of the lead hand faces the target at the finish.

Drills
Trail Arm Range of Motion

The following drill is to **test your individual range of motion** and provide a better understanding of the trail arm folding and unfolding.

Step 1

Stand upright with a club in the trail hand and the forearm horizontal to the ground.
Bend the wrist backward with the palm facing away from the body.

Step 2

Externally rotate the arm to your side at your maximum keeping the shaft vertical.

Drills
Trail Arm Range of Motion

Step 3

The **downswing begins by unfolding the trail elbow** to straighten the arm to your side.
(Wrist still bent)

Step 4

With **no wrist action**, slowly swing the arm through with the palm facing the target all the way to the finish.

Drills
Trail Arm Range of Motion

Step 5

Step 6

Palm facing the target at the finish and the wrist is still bent backward.

Drills
Trail Arm Movement

Knowing your arm range of motion allows you practice folding and unfolding within your limitation while in the setup position.

With the lead foot turned and the trail foot back, bend forward at the hips. Hand hooded with **the tip of the thumb on the target side of the grip and a soft elbow** (relaxed) to allow for an early fold on the takeaway.

Swing Position 1

Drills
Trail Arm Movement

The fold and unfold from the address setup position to the finish.

Swing Position 2

Swing Position 3

Drills
Trail Arm Movement

The fold and unfold from the address setup position to the finish.

Swing Position 4

Swing Position 5

Drills
Trail Arm Movement

The fold and unfold from the address setup position to the finish.

Swing Position 6

The swing momentum will pull you up out of your posture and into the finish.

Drills
Trail Arm Range of Motion

This drill is to allow you to feel the swing difference with the feet even / square to the toe line and with the trail foot back.

Feet Square to the toe line

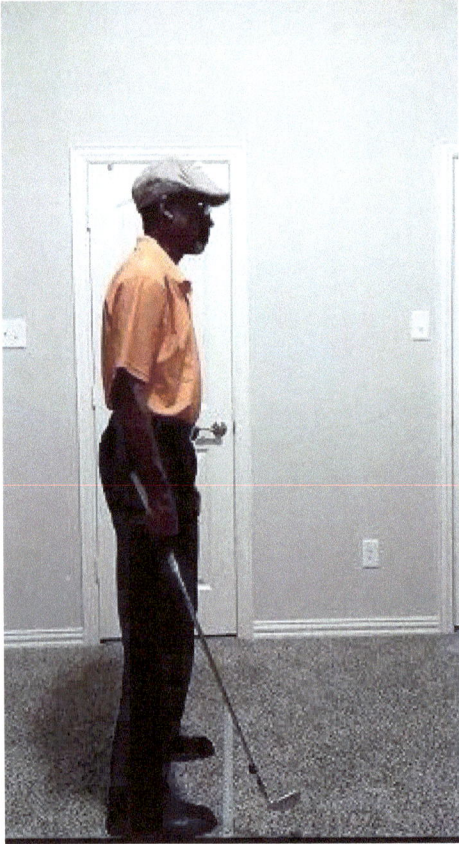

Step 1

Stand upright with your feet square to the toe line and a club in the trail hand.

Drills
Trail Arm Range of Motion
Feet Square to the toe line

Step 2

Bend the elbow with the forearm horizontal to the ground. Bend the wrist back with the palm facing away from the body to position the shaft vertical. **(Maintain this bent wrist position all the way to the finish)**

Drills
Trail Arm Range of Motion
Feet Square to the toe line

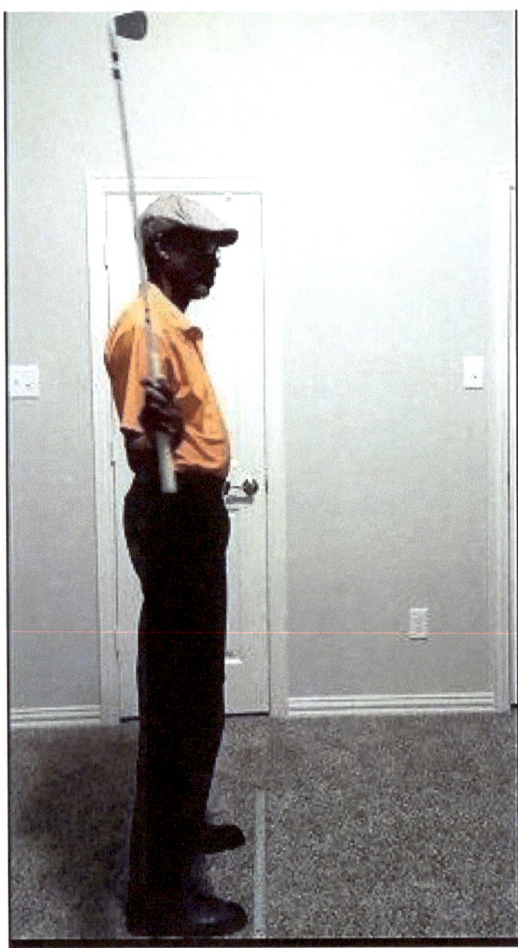

Step 3

Externally rotate the arm to your maximum keeping the shaft vertical.

Drills
Trail Arm Range of Motion
Feet Square to the toe line

Step 4

Bend forward at the hips keeping the shaft vertical.

Drills
Trail Arm Range of Motion
Feet Square to the toe line

Step 5

Extend the lead arm over and grip the club.

Drills
Trail Arm Range of Motion
Feet Square to the toe line

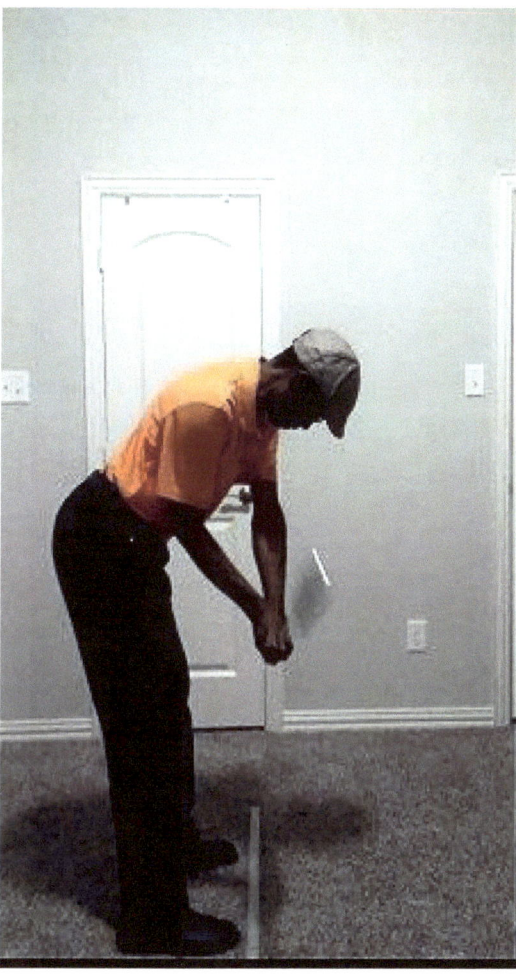

Step 6

Slowly swing forward by unfolding the trail elbow only.
(No wrist action)

Drills
Trail Arm Range of Motion
Feet Square to the toe line

Step 7

At post impact allow the lead elbow to start bending / folding.

Drills
Trail Arm Range of Motion
Feet Square to the toe line

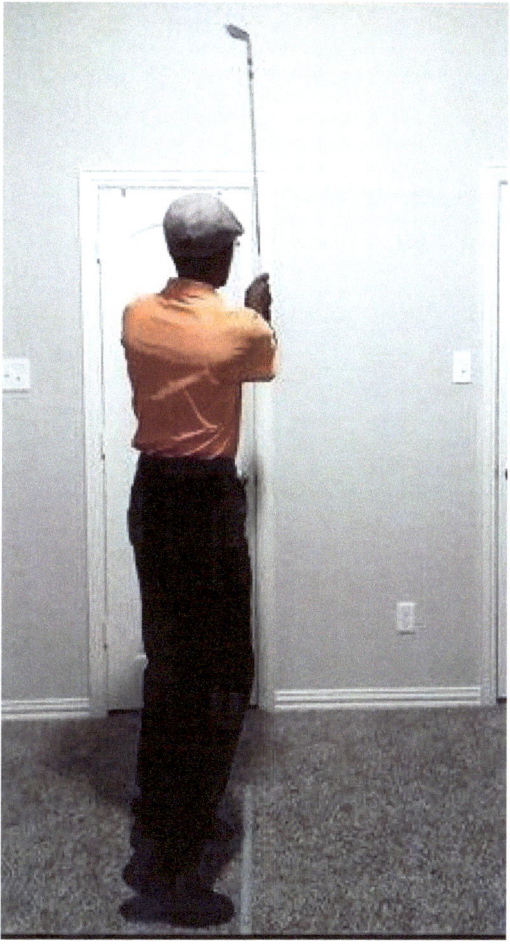

Step 8

Lead elbow bend will allow the shaft to go vertical and the back of the lead hand to face the target at the finish.
(Trail wrist still bent backward)

Drills
Trail Arm Range of Motion

Repeat the process, but this time drop the trail foot back from the toe line before you bend forward.

Take mental notes of any swing differences you see or feel.

Trail foot back from the toe line

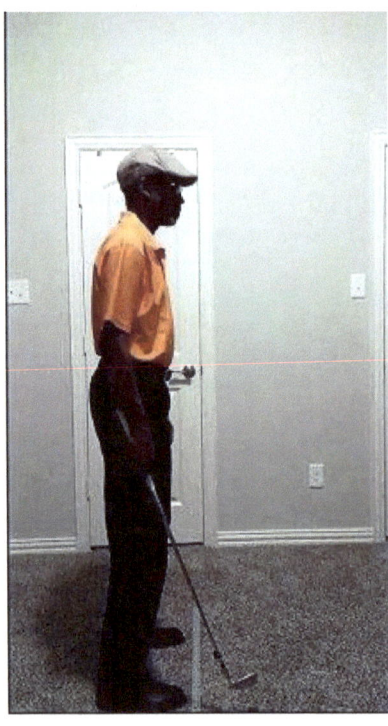

Step 1

Stand upright with your feet square to the toe line and a club in the trail hand.

Drills
Trail Arm Range of Motion
Trail foot back from the toe line

Step 2

Bend the elbow with the forearm horizontal to the ground. Bend the wrist back with the palm facing away from the body to position the shaft vertical. **(Maintain this bent wrist position all the way to the finish)**

Drills
Trail Arm Range of Motion
Trail foot back from the toe line

Step 3

Externally rotate the arm to your maximum keeping the shaft vertical.

Drills
Trail Arm Range of Motion
Trail foot back from the toe line

Step 4

Move the trail foot back from the toe line.

Drills
Trail Arm Range of Motion
Trail foot back from the toe line

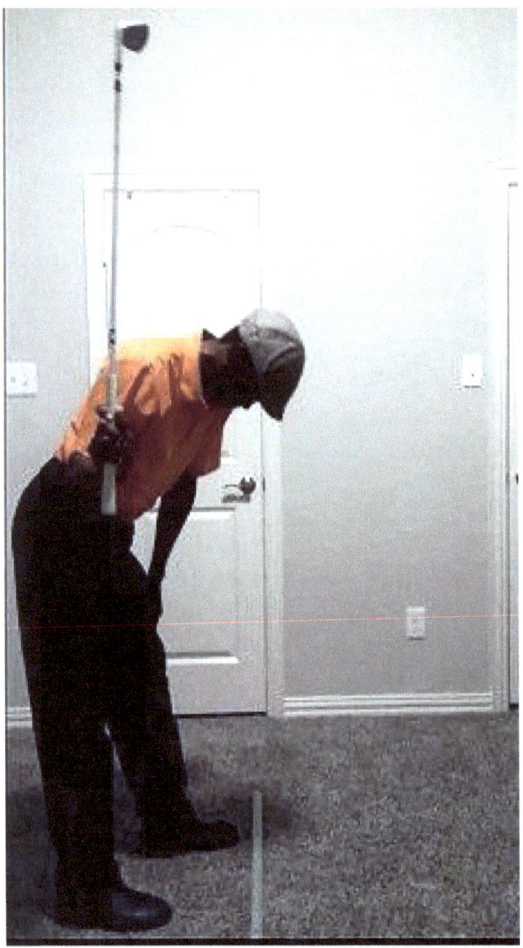

Step 5

Bend forward at the hips keeping the shaft vertical.

Drills
Trail Arm Range of Motion
Trail foot back from the toe line

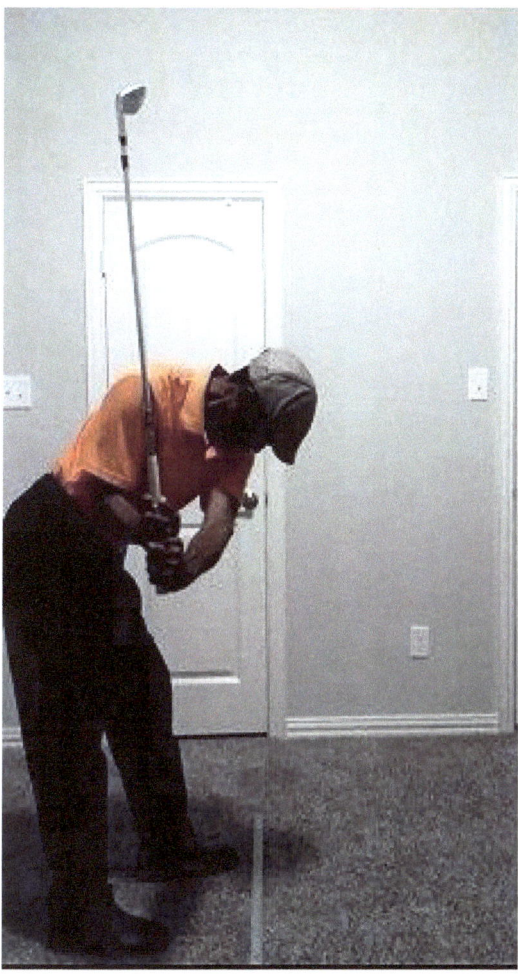

Step 6

Extend the lead arm over and grip the club.

Drills
Trail Arm Range of Motion
Trail foot back from the toe line

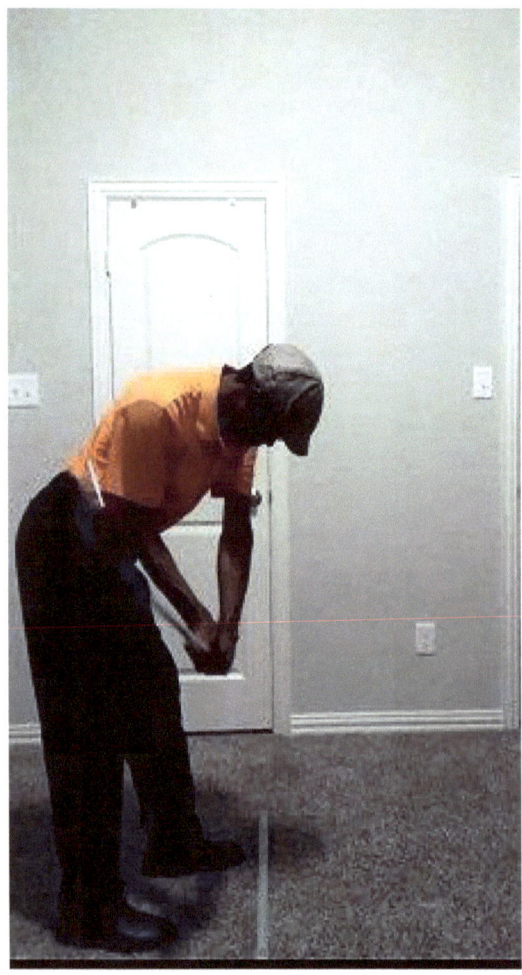

Step 7

Slowly swing forward by unfolding the trail elbow only.
(No wrist action)

Drills
Trail Arm Range of Motion
Trail foot back from the toe line

Step 8

At post impact allow the lead elbow to start bending / folding.

Drills
Trail Arm Range of Motion
Trail foot back from the toe line

Step 9

Lead elbow bend will allow the shaft to go vertical and the back of the lead hand to face the target at the finish.
(Trail wrist still bent backward)

Drills

The following drills can be performed indoors or outside with or without a golf club to help you better understand and perfect the swing movements.

Lead Arm Seated

Allow the Lead elbow to begin folding / bending at post impact (position #5) so that the back of the hand faces the target on the finish (position #6).

Drills
Lead Arm Seated

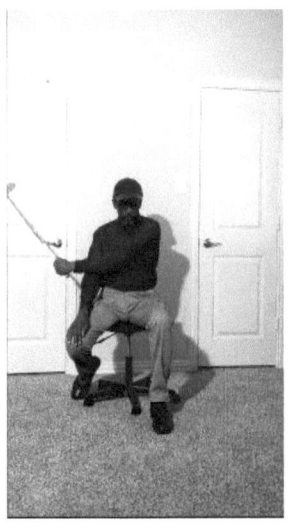

Allow the Lead elbow to begin folding / bending at post impact (position #5) so that the back of the hand faces the target on the finish (position #6).

Drills
Trail Arm Seated

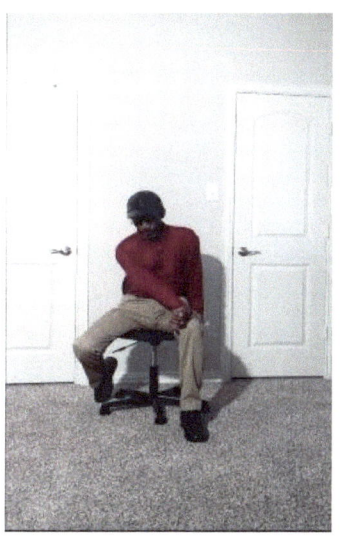

Touch the tip of the thumb to the tip of the forefinger. Bend the wrist back; rotate the forearm internally and rest the wrist on the lead thigh. Relax the elbow then fold and unfold the elbow with no wrist action.
(Maintain the pre-set wrist angle from address to the finish)

Drills
Trail Arm Seated

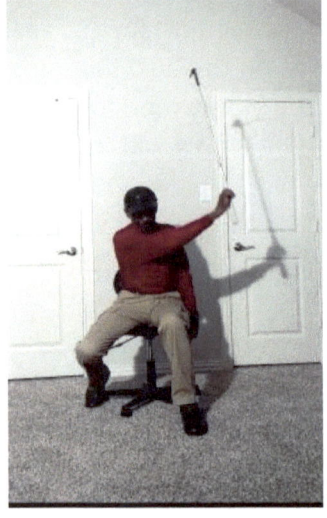

Grip down on a club for leverage.
Bend the wrist back; rotate the forearm internally and rest the wrist on the lead thigh.
Relax the elbow then fold and unfold the elbow with no wrist action.
(Maintain the pre-set wrist angle from address to the finish)

Drills
Both Arms Seated

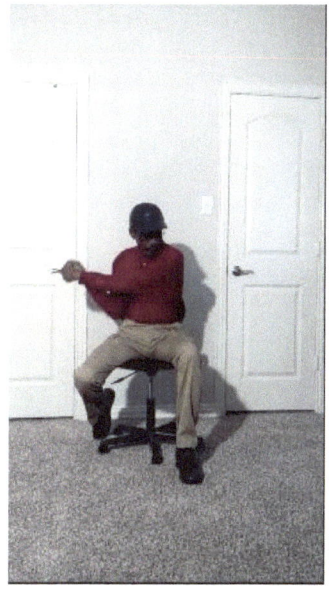

Rest the lead wrist on the lead thigh with the thumb up. With the trail hand grasp the lead thumb as gripping a club. Relax the trail elbow then fold and unfold the elbow with no wrist action.
(Maintain the pre-set wrist angle from address to the finish)

Drills
Both Arms Seated

Grip a club and rest the hands on the lead thigh.
Relax the trail elbow then fold and unfold the elbow with no wrist action.
(Maintain the pre-set wrist angle from address to the finish)

Drills
Both Arms Standing

With the trail hand grasp the lead thumb as gripping a club. Get into the address setup position.

Relax the trail elbow then fold and unfold the elbow with no wrist action.

(Maintain the pre-set wrist angle from address to the finish)

Allow the swing momentum to bring you out of posture and up into the finish.

Drills
Both Arms Standing

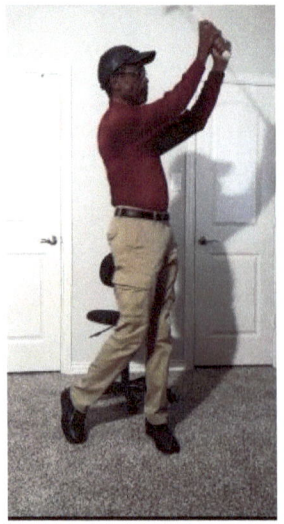

Grip a club and get into the address setup position.

Relax the trail elbow then fold and unfold the elbow with no wrist action.

(Maintain the pre-set wrist angle from address to the finish)

Allow the swing momentum to bring you out of posture and up into the finish.

Drills
Half Shaft

This drill will allow you to see and feel the end of the grip tracing the path of the swing.

Swing Position 0

Grip the club half way down the shaft.

Swing Position 1

Fold the Trail elbow with no wrist action.

Drills
Half Shaft

Swing Position 2

Swing Position 3

Drills
Half Shaft

Swing Position 4

Unfold the Trail elbow with no wrist action.
(Maintain the pre-set wrist angle from address to the finish)

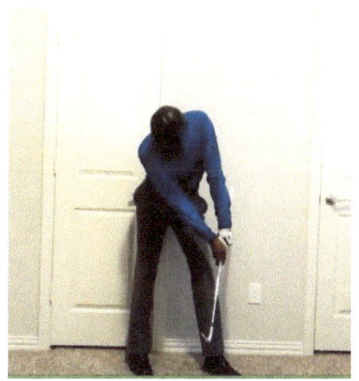

Swing Position 5

Swing Position 6

Allow the Lead elbow to begin folding / bending at post impact *(position #5)* **so that the back of the hand faces the target on the finish** *(position #6)***.**

Drills

The balance drills will help you to maintain perfect balance with 70% weight on the lead leg for putting and chipping.

Putting Balance

Grip the putter in the lead hand with the trail arm behind your back.

Balance on the lead foot turned toward the target with the trail foot back from the toe line and heel slightly off the ground.

Drills
Putting Balance

Swing back and through with a lead arm pendulum stroke.

Drills
Chipping Balance

Grip the club in the lead hand with the trail arm behind your back.

Balance on the lead foot turned toward the target with the trail foot back from the toe line and heel slightly off the ground.

Drills
Chipping Balance

Swing back and down through the low point with a lead arm pendulum swing to post impact.

Drills
Swing Path

Perform this drill with your eyes closed to subconsciously see and feel the path of the swing.

Lead arm only without a club.

From the address setup position allow the lead arm to hang down in front of the thigh with the trail hand behind your back or on your hip.

Visualize the toe line extending up vertical and dissecting the body somewhere in the area of the trail ear or neck.
(Yellow "**X**")

Drills
Swing Path

From the setup position to when the hand is approaching hip high, **the feel should be up toward the ear**.

At the end of the backswing **the feel is that the hand has naturally moved toward the tip of the shoulder and on the inside to out path**, so all that is required is to allow it to drop straight down.

Drills
Swing Path

Drills
Swing Path

Drills
Swing Path

Both arms without a club.

From the address setup position allow the lead arm to hang down in front of the thigh then grasp the thumb with **the trail hand hooded and a soft elbow**.

Starting the takeaway with the trail thumb will allow for an early fold of the elbow so that the hands go up toward the ear.

Drills
Swing Path

At the end of the backswing **the hands are naturally on the inside to out path**.

Initiate the downswing with the unfolding of the trail elbow, allowing the hands to drop straight down to your side.

Drills
Swing Path

The swing will zip through the impact zone then out and up to the target apex.

Drills
Swing Path

Lead arm only with a club.

Drills
Swing Path

Drills
Swing Path

Drills
Swing Path

Both arm with a club.

Drills
Swing Path

Drills
Swing Path

Final Thought

Now that you have made preparations to play a game that can be played for a lifetime.

Remember that Life is not a game to be played.

It is now time to make preparation for Life Eternal.

For God so loved the world, that He gave his only begotten Son, that whosoever believeth in him should not perish, but have everlasting life. (John 3:16)

That if thou shalt confess with thy mouth the Lord Jesus, and shalt believe in thine heart that God hath raised him from the dead, thou shalt be saved. For with the heart man believeth unto righteousness; and with the mouth confession is made unto salvation.
Romans 10:9-10

Jesus is the Only Way
John 14:6

Truth will be revealed when you accept
Jesus Christ as Savior and LORD.

Glossary

Booster Muscle – the trail shoulder deltoid muscle.

Grip Pressure scale – 1 = very light
                       10 = tight as possible

Hood – is a bent (flexed) trail wrist with the forearm internally rotated to the individual's maximum.

Lead Side – the side of the body that is closer to the target at the setup position. (i.e., lead arm, lead leg and lead foot)

Soft Elbow – slightly bent elbow

Trail Side – the side of the body that is farther from the target at the setup position. (i.e., trail arm, trail leg and trail foot)

www.ingramcontent.com/pod-product-compliance
Lightning Source LLC
Chambersburg PA
CBHW042304150426
43197CB00001B/11